MY DOG
MAY BE
A GENIUS

drawings by
JAMES STEVENSON

poems by
JACK PRELUTSKY

MY DOG
MAY BE
A GENIUS

GREENWILLOW BOOKS
An Imprint of HarperCollinsPublishers

Pen and ink were used to prepare the art.
The text type is Optima.

Library of Congress Cataloging-in-Publication Data
Prelutsky, Jack.
My dog may be a genius: poems / by Jack Prelutsky;
pictures by James Stevenson.
  p. cm.
"Greenwillow Books."
ISBN: 978-0-06-623862-3 (trade bdg.)
ISBN: 978-0-06-623863-0 (lib. bdg.)
1. Children's poetry, American. I. Stevenson,
James, (date) ill. II. Title.
PS3566.R36M89 2008 811'.54—dc22 2007019462

First Edition 10 9 8 7 6 5 4 3 2 1
Greenwillow Books

For Izzy Young, my good old friend

My Dog May Be a Genius

My dog may be a genius,
and in fact, there's little doubt.
He recognizes many words,
unless I spell them out.
If I so much as whisper *"walk,"*
he hurries off at once
to fetch his leash . . . it's evident
my dog is not a dunce.

I can't say *"food"* in front of him,
I spell *f-o-o-d,*
and he goes wild unless I spell
his *t-r-e-a-t.*
But recently this tactic
isn't working out too well.
I think my *d-o-g* has learned
to *s-p-e-l-l.*

Please Let Me Sleep All Day Today

Please let me sleep all day today,
I need to stay in bed.
I'm hardly even half awake,
I'm sure my eyes are red.

I try and try to open them,
but can't remember how.
You say today is Saturday?
I'm getting up right now.

The Underwater Marching Band

We're the members of the famous
Underwater Marching Band,
renowned for never having played
a single sound on land.
We blare away with gusto
and unmitigated cheer,
undaunted by the knowledge
we're impossible to hear.

We're utterly incapable
of ever being heard,
and yet we're undiscouraged,
undismayed, and undeterred.
Despite our insufficiency,
we're disinclined to fret—
we're the **Underwater Marching Band**,
perennially wet.

Two Penguins Once Collided

Two penguins once collided—
both were in a nasty mood
and quickly started bickering . . .
they were extremely rude.

Those penguins argued on and on
without an interlude,
and that was the beginning
of their famous frozen feud.

The Zeenaleens

The Zeenaleens are fond of beans
and often eat a pound.
It isn't very difficult
to tell when they're around.

If they are in your neighborhood,
you're guaranteed to find them.
It's best to meet them face to face—
don't *ever* stand behind them.

I Know You Won't Believe Me

I know you won't believe me,
it must sound strange to you,
but, teacher, what I'm saying
is absolutely true.
I worked on my assignment,
it took me half the night.
I answered every question,
and think I got some right.

As soon as I was finished,
I left it on my chair,
but when I woke this morning,
my homework wasn't there.
My sister hadn't taken it,
she told me I was weird.
My mother simply shrugged to hear
that it had disappeared.

I rummaged through the closets,
the kitchen, and the den,
expecting that my homework
would soon be seen again.
But when I saw the ashes,
you should have heard me shriek—
my dragon burned my homework,
just like he did last week.

A Letter from Camp

My counselor says I have to write—
I threw up on my sweater.
I had the runs again last night,
my rash is getting better.
I accidentally scared a skunk,
a hornet stung my head.
I'm sleeping in a lower bunk,
my bunkmate wets the bed.

They had to shave off all my hair,
I've got a stomach cramp.
I don't have any underwear,
my socks are mostly damp.
I fell out of another tree,
and here's a bug I found.
I love it here. So long.
                    Love,
                    Me
P.S. I almost drowned.

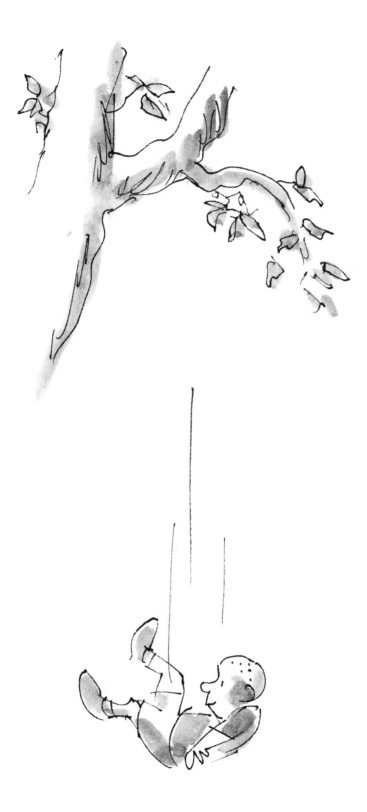

I'm Not Afraid of Anything

I'm not afraid of anything,
except, perhaps, of bears,
and spiders, snakes, and centipedes,
and falling down the stairs.
I'm slightly apprehensive
I'll be swallowed by a shark,
and tend to run for cover
when it thunders in the dark.

It's possible I'm just a bit
uncomfortable with bats,
or spending my vacation
with a pack of savage rats.
If I were lost in outer space,
I might feel weird inside,
and if I spied a dragon,
there's a likelihood I'd hide.

I shy away from lions,
and from tigers just as well,
and I avoid all witches,
lest they cast a dreadful spell.
I think I'd rather never meet
an ogre, ten feet tall—
but I am not the least afraid
of anything at all.

I Thought I Saw

I thought I saw **BBBBBBBBBB**
dive down into the **CCCCCCC**.
Could I believe my own **II**?
I'm not so sure, I'm not **YY**.

The Leaves Are Turning Colors

The leaves are turning colors,
and dropping from the trees.
They float and swirl and flutter,
they dance upon the breeze.

They're amber, red, and yellow,
they make a lovely sight,
and if it weren't summer,
then that would be all right.

The View from Here

The view from here is very strange,
the porcupines are flying.
The crocodiles are laughing,
and the kangaroos are crying.
A bobolink is bouncing
on a tiny trampoline,
a panda's flipping pancakes—
it's no ordinary scene.

An elephant is singing,
and a donkey does a dance.
An octopus is juggling
a variety of plants.
A centipede is sneezing
in an armadillo's ear,
and storks are turning somersaults—
I like the view from here.

Crumbo Crumme

I'm Crumbo Crumme, I'm always glum,
that simply is my style.
I sit and mope, and there's no hope
I'll crack the slightest smile.
You can't begin to make me grin
or change my attitude.
There's nothing you can ever do
to elevate my mood.

Try tickling me, and soon you'll see,
it doesn't change a thing,
and songs of cheer are wasted here—
I won't join in and sing.
There is no tune that you can croon
that I will even hum.
Save all your jokes for other folks,
but not for Crumbo Crumme.

I'm in a Muddy Puddle

I'm in a muddy puddle,
and attempting to escape,
but the puddle won't permit me—
I'm in catastrophic shape.
If I'd watched where I was going,
I would not be in distress,
but I didn't pay attention,
so I'm in a muddy mess.

The harder that I struggle here,
the more I seem to sink.
I cannot extricate myself,
and don't know what to think.
My only hope is calling out,
I'll yell and yell and yell—
Perhaps I'll soon be rescued,
but if I'm not . . . farewell!

I Peered in a Mirror

I peered in a mirror,
the mirror fell down.
I glanced at my shadow,
it sped out of town.

I watched my reflection
swim off in the sea—
there's something peculiar
today about me.

A Skunk Sat in a Courtroom

A skunk sat in a courtroom.
A judge was on the bench.
He held his nose and shouted,
"What is that dreadful stench?"

"It's only me, Your Honor,"
the skunk said in retort.
"I thought I heard you calling
for odor in the court."

Sarah, Sarah

Sarah, Sarah, why so sour,
you've been sour all day long,
oh so sour, every hour,
sour Sarah, what is wrong?

Sarah, please don't glare and glower,
even for a little while.
Sarah, Sarah, don't be sour,
sour Sarah, won't you smile?

C
I
T
N
A
G
I
G

I drank
a magic
potion,
the effect
was very
weird.
At first I grew

now
I've
almost
d
i
s
a
p
p
e
a
r
e
d.

I Crossed a Lion with a Mouse

I crossed a lion with a mouse.
Their progeny patrol my house,
and often roar, demanding cheese—
I give them all the cheese they please.

I'm Shopping for a Dinosaur

I'm shopping for a dinosaur.
I'd like one small enough
to fit into my backpack
that's already filled with stuff.
I don't want one with pointy teeth,
or claws of any kind.
The dinosaur I'm looking for
is difficult to find.

I'm shopping for a dinosaur,
and hunting all around.
So far I'm unsuccessful,
it is nowhere to be found.
I hear they disappeared before
the year that I was born.
I'm giving up on dinosaurs—
I'll buy a unicorn.

On Monday at Midnight

On Monday at midnight, my griffin and I
rise through the clouds to an ebony sky.
I straddle his back, and I cling very tight.
He flexes his wings, and we soar out of sight.

We silently, swiftly, ascend in the air,
a magic, miraculous aerial pair.
We're all by ourselves as we hover and glide,
the moon is our lantern, the stars are our guide.

My griffin is strong, and with infinite ease,
he carries me high over mountains and seas.
As soon as I tug on his mane with my hand,
my griffin defers to my slightest command.

But when the sun rises, my griffin, instead,
deposits me tenderly back in my bed.
In barely a week, once again we will fly . . .
on Monday at midnight, my griffin and I.

Because I Don't Like Lima Beans

Because I don't like lima beans,
I dropped them in my juice.
My mother noticed what I did,
and so it was no use.
I slyly set my spinach,
on the floor beneath my chair.
My mother's eyes are very sharp,
she saw it sitting there.

I tried to hide my broccoli
behind the window shade.
My mother gave it back to me,
I was a bit dismayed.
Whenever I hide vegetables,
she finds them in a blink.
It's hard to fool my mother—
she knows the way I think.

A Bear Is Not Disposed

A bear is not disposed
to dressing up in clothes,
not even underwear—
a bear likes being bare.

My Parents Gave Me Birthday Gifts

My parents gave me birthday gifts
I didn't want at all.
I would have loved a scooter,
or a brand-new basketball.
Instead they gave me handkerchiefs
for which I do not care,
a hat with silly earflaps
that I hope I never wear.

I opened up one package,
and I think I almost cried
when I saw the purple sweater
that was lying there inside.
I also got an awful pair
of monogrammed pajamas,
a book on punctuation marks
like periods and commas.

They gave me lots of ugly socks
I do not like a bit,
a stupid comb and brush set—
I am not too fond of it.
They might as well have given me
a bucketful of rain,
but since it's not my birthday,
I'm not going to complain.

I Am Gooboo

I am Gooboo, who are you?
Can you do what I can do?
I can drink the largest lake,
make the ground beneath me quake.
I can juggle tons of trees,
or a billion bumblebees,
run a hundred thousand miles,
wrestle ninety crocodiles.

There is no one else like me.
I can swim across the sea,
even swallow half the sky
while I hoist a hippo high.
I can dance upon the sun,
dive back down when I am done,
chew the universe in two . . .
I am Gooboo, who are you?

My Pig Put On a Bathing Suit

My pig put on a bathing suit
and headed for the shore,
then sat beneath the blazing sun
from ten till ten to four.

Of course it soon was sunburned,
all its tender skin was sore.
I covered it with *oinkment* . . .
my pig is sore no more.

I Often Mow the Bathtub

I often mow the bathtub,
and I bathe upon the grass.
I often fish for horses,
and I saddle up a bass.
Sometimes I hammer my guitar,
sometimes I strum a nail.
Sometimes I sort my breakfast
while I eat the morning mail.

Before I climb on water,
I may swim a flight of stairs.
Before I nibble basketballs,
I dribble plums and pears.
Although I shovel bowling pins,
I also juggle dirt,
and when I wear a pizza,
I may also bake a shirt.

I like to shine potatoes,
and I like to mash my shoes.
Before I read my bicycle,
I like to ride the news.
I've tried to ring a tiger,
and I've tried to tame a bell.
My days are always interesting,
as surely you can tell.

Beezil B. Bone

I'm Beezil B. Bone,
I live under a stone.
I fully prefer
that you leave me alone.
Don't bother to knock,
I won't answer your call—
I'd rather not make
your acquaintance at all.

I'm Beezil B. Bone,
an unsavory elf.
I like being left
to my miserable self.
Your presence offends me,
so please, go away.
If you've any sense,
then you'll do as I say.

I'm likely to bite,
and you'll know when I do.
My fangs are so sharp
they'll go right through your shoe.
You'll hop up and down,
and you'll shriek and you'll moan. . . .
I'm Beezil B. Bone,
I live under a stone.

If You Were a Rhinoceros

If you were a rhinoceros,
I still would be your friend.
And if you were a platypus,
our friendship would not end.
I'd like you as a walrus,
camel, cat, or kangaroo.
It doesn't matter what you are—
I'll still be friends with you.

Boys Are Big Experts

Boys are big experts
at looking for trouble,
they climb over fences,
they tunnel through rubble.
Boys take their time
when they're called to the table,
boys love to eat
like they lived in a stable.

Boys tend to throw things
and get into tussles,
make nasty noises,
and show off their muscles,
lots of stuff leading
to bruises and bleeding—
why don't they stop for a while . . .
and start READING?

Sandwich Stan

I'm Sandwich Stan, the sandwich man,
and in my sandwich shop,
I make amazing sandwiches,
impossible to top.
To show you why my patrons
are enthralled by every bite,
I offer here a sampling
that will tempt your appetite.

ALMOND APPLE ALLIGATOR

BARRACUDA BAKED IN BRINE

SCRAMBLED BUGS FROM THE EQUATOR

KNITTING NEEDLE KNOTTY PINE

CREAM OF CALAMARI CANDLE

BADGER BELLY BOILED IN BILE

SALTED SALAMANDER SANDAL

RUTABAGA ROOFING TILE

PHILODENDRON PHEASANT FEATHER

TURTLE TENDON TUNA TAILS

LICHEN LEMON LIZARD LEATHER

SCALDED ARMADILLO SCALES

CRICKET CATERPILLAR CRAYON

MANTIS MANGO MAGGOT MOLD

RANCID RADISH WRAPPED IN RAYON

SPARROW MARROW MARIGOLD

BEETLE BEET BANANA BLUBBER

CHIGGER CHEESE CHINCHILLA CHALK

RHODODENDRON ROTTEN RUBBER

CRISPY GRISTLE THISTLE STALK

ANTS AND CANTALOUPE WITH NOODLES

FERRET FAT IN MOSSY MUCK

PICKLED PELTS OF PUGS AND POODLES

JALAPEÑO HOCKEY PUCK

At my singular establishment
my customers adore
the sandwiches I fashion
and keep clamoring for more.
So hurry to my sandwich shop
if you're a sandwich fan.
You won't be disappointed here . . .
my name is Sandwich Stan.

The Snabbit

The Snabbit has a habit
that I do not like a bit.
It sneaks behind me silently,
then bites me where I sit.

That Snabbit has the equally
annoying little knack
of vanishing before I've time
to bite its backside back.

I Have a Rat

I have a rat, my rat is nice.
It's twice as nice as toads or mice.
It likes to sit atop my head,
and snuggle up all night in bed.

Its fur is gray, its nose is pink.
It's handsome for a rat, I think,
so I don't know the reason that
my mother cannot stand my rat.

My Current Situation

My current situation
is ostensibly unique.
Alarming things are happening
to alter my physique.
I'm growing hooves, I have a tail,
my neck now sports a mane,
and I can hardly wait to graze
upon a grassy plain.

My ears are getting longer,
I have stripes of black and white.
I'm clearly in the midst
of an unprecedented plight.
My face is unfamiliar,
and my body's fully furred.
I feel a sudden urgency
to join a zebra herd.

My posture is devolving,
now I'm standing on all fours,
and I'm becoming more afraid
of anything that roars.
My equine transformation
is indubitably done.
I sense a stalking lioness . . .
I think I'd better run.

My Family's Unconventional

My family's unconventional
in almost every way.
We demonstrate this perfectly
on Independence Day.

We butter up our noses
on the fourth day of July.
It's a family tradition—
we simply don't know why.

A Table Saw a Cow Hide

A table saw a cow hide,
but the cow was unaware
it was under observation,
that the table saw it there.

A seesaw saw the incident,
and telephoned the law,
who arrested both the bovine
and the nosy table saw.

One Day in the Woods

Some wondrous things happened
one day in the woods,
the wolves blew their whistles,
the robins wore hoods.
A pig told a tale
to a toad on a stool,
the lynx got too hot,
but the leopard stayed cool.

52

The eagles played harps,
and the rabbits played jacks,
the beavers seemed bored
with the talkative yaks.
The turtles all turned
and the turkeys soon froze,
a horse lost its voice,
and the bears lost their clothes.

The skunks were incensed
that the swifts were too slow,
the monkeys were gleaming,
the worms were aglow.
The bison were baffled,
the rats ran a race . . .
one day in the woods
all these wonders took place.

An Enigmatic Entity

An enigmatic entity
is floating by my head.
It first appeared last weekend,
as I tumbled out of bed.
It's not a bit impressive,
just a fuzzy little sphere.
I can't imagine what it wants,
or what it's doing here.

It's an eerie apparition
that has yet to make a sound.
I sense that I'm the only one
who knows that it's around.
It's somewhat reassuring,
with a certain quiet charm.
As far as I can figure out,
it clearly means no harm.

When I'm awake, that entity
is never out of sight,
and I suspect it's also there
when I'm asleep at night.
I've grown to like it, so I hope
I never see the day
that enigmatic entity
decides to float away.

A Silly Sheep

A silly sheep, whose morning meal,
instead of grass, was flecks of steel,
consumed a total bellyful,
and grew a coat of pure steel wool.

Call of the Long-winded Clumsy Owl

WHOOOOOOOOOOOOOOOOOOOOOOOOOOOOOOOOOOOOOOOO
OOOOOOOOOOOOOOOOOOOOOOOOOOOOOOOOOOOOOOOOOO
OOOOOOOOOOOOOOOOOOOOOOOOOOOOOOOOOOOOOOOOOO
OOOOOOOOOOOOOOOOOOOOOOOOOOOOOOOOOOOOOOOOOO
OOOOOOOOOOOOOOOOOOOOOOOOOOOOOOOOOOOOOOOOOO
OOOOOOOOOOOOOOOOOOOOOOOOOOOOOOOOOOOOOOOOOO
OOOOOOOOOOOOOOOOOOOOOOOOOOOOOOOOOOOOOOOOOO
OOOOOOOOOOOOOOOOOOOOOOOOOOOOOOOOOOOOOOOOOO
OOOOOOOOOOOOOOOOOOOOOOOOOOOOOOOOOOOOOOOOOO
OOOOOOOOOOOOOOOOOOOOOOOOOOOOOOOOOOOOOOOOOO
OOOOOOOOOOOOOOOOOOOOOOOOOOOOOOOOOOOOOOOOOO
OOOOOOOOOOOOOOOOOOOOOOOOOOOOOOOOOOOOOOOOOO
OOOOOOOOOOOOOOOOOOOOOOOOOOOOOOOOOOOOOOOOOO
OOOOOOOOOOOOOOOOOOOOOOOOOOOOOOOOOOOOOOOOOO
OOOOOOOOOOOOOOOOOOOOOOOOOOOOOOOOOOOOOOOOOO
OOOOOOOOOOOOOOOOOOOOOOOOOOOOOOOOOOOOOOOOOO
OOOOOOOOOOOOOOOOOOOOOOOOOOOOOOOOOOOOOOOOOO
OOOOOOOOOOOOOOOOOOOOOOOOOOOOOOOOOOOOOOOOOO
OOOOOOOOOOOOOOOOOOOOOOOOOOOOOOOOOOOOOOOOOO
OOOOOOOOOOOOOOOOOOOOOOOOOOOOOOOOOOOOOOOOOO
OOOOOOOOOOOOOOOOOOOOOOOOOOOOOOOOOOOOOOOOOO
OOOOOOOOOOOOOOOOOOOOOOOOOOOOOOOOOOOOOOOOOO
OOOOOOOOOOOOOOOOOOOOOOOOOOOOOOOOOOOOOOOPS!

57

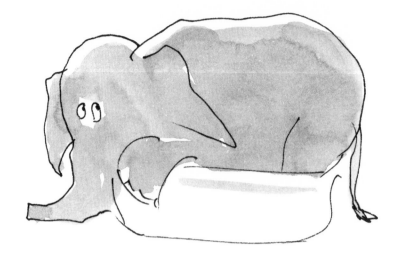

My Absentminded Elephant

My absentminded elephant
is odder than most pets.
It simply can't remember much,
it constantly forgets.
It tends to waste a lot of time
attempting to recall
what elephants should keep in mind—
it still forgets it all.

It used to balance on a ball,
it used to take a bow,
but now it doesn't do these things,
it can't remember how.
It loses lots of peanuts,
plus a host of other things.
It tries to fly, forgetting
that it hasn't any wings.

It regularly takes a bath,
forgetting, there's no doubt,
it's bigger than our bathtub,
so we have to pry it out.
It even has forgotten
it was frightened of our mouse . . .
it's hard to keep an elephant
like that around the house.

Two Dozen of My Words

TWO DOZEN OF MY WORDS

WERE PECKED APART BY BIRDS,

AND NOW THEY TAKE

MORE TIME TO READ,

FOR THEY ARE ALL IN THIRDS.

I Wished into a Wishing Well

I wished into a wishing well,
my wishes were in vain.
I tried to catch a rainbow,
but it vanished like the rain.

I dug for buried treasure
till my shovel came apart.
I heard a rhyme inside my head,
and now it's in my heart.

When Ozzie Snozzer Sneezes

When Ozzie Snozzer sneezes,
an extraordinary sound
departs his ample nostrils,
and resounds for miles around.
It's louder than the honking
of a crowd of rowdy geese.
Some people hide in horror,
others summon the police.

That sneeze is unendurable,
and flusters dogs and cats.
It startles frogs, unsettles fish,
and rouses drowsy bats.
Birds dart about, abandoning
the comfort of the nest,
though at the zoo, the elephants
are patently impressed.

The sky turns dark and menacing,
the sun appears to dim,
as clouds unloose a torrent . . .
it's all because of him.
The planet often wobbles
in a disconcerting way
when Ozzie Snozzer sneezes—
and he sneezes every day.

63

I Am on a Bumpy Road

I am on a bumpy road, I've been on it for a while. I bet me wish I'd never wandered from the avenue. I watch my every step, there's no question that I must, for when I don't, more. It's hard to stay alert when my feet just hurt and hurt, so my progress has inevitably slowed. How I hope, around the bend,

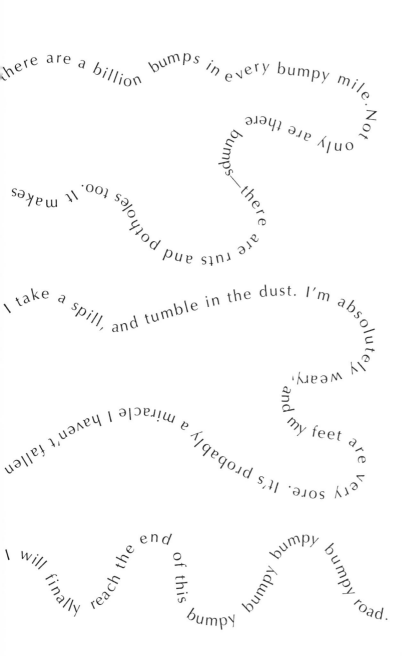

there are a billion bumps in every bumpy mile. Not only are there bumps—there are ruts and potholes too. It makes I take a spill, and tumble in the dust. I'm absolutely weary, and my feet are very sore. It's probably a miracle I haven't fallen I will finally reach the end of this bumpy bumpy bumpy bumpy road.

Winterwood

I am Winterwood, a wizard
steeped in necromantic lore.
I can levitate your body
fifty feet above the floor.
If I wish, you are a piglet
overeating at a trough,
or a pirouetting robot
with no switch to turn you off.

I am Winterwood, a weaver
of abominable spells.
With a waggle of my whiskers,
I can rearrange your cells.
If I choose you as my victim,
you will find you can't prevent
the unpleasant consequences
of my terrible intent.

I continually revel
in disreputable deeds,
changing children into chickens,
lovely roses into weeds.
When I fly into a frenzy,
you'll do well to feel alarm.
I am Winterwood, a wizard . . .
there's a chance I mean you harm.

I'm Sitting Doing Nothing

I'm sitting doing nothing,
which I do extremely well.
Exactly how I do it
is impossible to tell.
I scarcely move a muscle,
but serenely stay in place,
not even slightly changing
the expression on my face.

I'm fond of doing nothing,
so I do it all day long.
Whenever I do nothing,
I don't ever do it wrong.
When I am doing nothing,
there is nothing that I do,
for if I started something,
it would mean that I was through.

When I am doing nothing,
I'm immobile as a wall.
When I am doing nothing,
I don't do a thing at all.
It's easy doing nothing
and I find it lots of fun,
though when I'm finally finished
I'm uncertain that I'm done.

Homework, Sweet Homework

Homework, sweet homework,
you heavenly thing,
as soon as I see you
I dance and I sing.
There's nothing on Earth
that I care about more
than homework, sweet homework,
the work I adore.

There's no better way
to spend most of my time
than doing that homework
I think is sublime.
I have a suspicion
I'd always be blue
if I had no homework,
sweet homework to do.

Homework, sweet homework,
how lovely you are,
I'd take you along
if I flew to a star.
My friends think I'm loony
to take such delight
in homework, sweet homework—
they're probably right.

I Wanted Macaroni

I wanted macaroni,
and ate eleven bowls,
and then a dozen doughnuts,
including all the holes.

I ate a hundred onions,
and wept a salty tide.
I ate two dozen carrots—
I'm solid gold inside.

A Turtle

A turtle never feels the need
to ambulate at breakneck speed.
Of course, unsuited for the deed,
it certainly would not succeed.

Because a turtle takes its time,
its life is quietly sublime.
It's happy in its habitat . . .
there's something to be said for that.

My Mouse Is Out

My mouse is out, my mouse is out,
it's scooting through the house.
It managed to escape its cage—
it's clever . . . for a mouse.
It waited till I went to bed,
then softly, while I slept,
it engineered its freedom . . .
it's ingenious and adept.

That rodent is resourceful,
and unwilling to be caught.
It's possibly the smartest mouse
that I have ever bought.
My sisters and my brothers
are assisting in the chase,
but my mouse is too elusive
as it darts from place to place.

So far our finest efforts
haven't been of any use.
My mouse is keen, and capable
of staying on the loose.
It's taking full advantage
of the fact that it's so small—
it's fled beneath the sofa,
where we cannot reach at all.

My mother's shrieking in alarm,
and bolting from the house.
"I won't be back," she's promising,
"until you catch that mouse."
I hope we catch it very soon,
though it's no easy chore,
for even though I love my mouse,
I love my mother more.

I Wakened This Morning

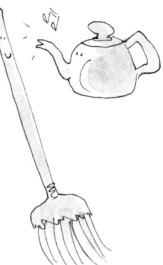

I wakened this morning at seven o'clock
and knew from the start I was in for a shock.
I couldn't help hearing, right there in my room,
the teakettle whistle a tune to the broom.

I looked out the window, and saw in the sky,
an ox and an octopus sauntering by.
The sun was bright blue, and the moon wore a crown,
the stars were still out, and they bounced up and down.

A gaggle of ganders was dancing a waltz,
as oysters were turning adroit somersaults.
Begonias were marching on gala parade,
while robins applauded and drank lemonade.

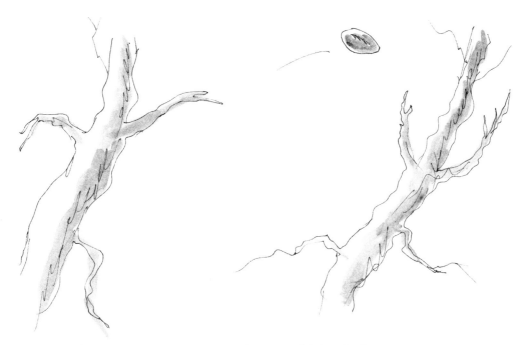

The trees were engaged in a wild football game,
they lacked any feet, but they played all the same—
whenever this happens, I know right away
it's going to be an unusual day.

A Fox Has Caught the Chickens

A fox has caught the chickens,
but the chickens fixed the fox.
That fox is skipping dinner,
for they gave him chicken pox.

A Fish in School

A fish in school is fortunate,
its life is trouble free.
It doesn't do arithmetic
or learn geography.

It hasn't any homework,
and it never carries books.
A fish in school just has to watch
for bigger fish . . . and hooks.

A Witch Was in a Hardware Store

A witch was in a hardware store,
she radiated gloom.
A clerk asked, "May I help you?"
She replied, "I've lost my broom!
I had that broom for ages,"
she continued through her tears.
"I must replace it right away,
for midnight quickly nears."

The clerk said, sympathetically,
"I'm sorry for your plight.
However, we sell splendid brooms,
you'll have one by tonight."
He added, "Let me show you some,"
and led her through the store.
"Our newest brooms sweep cleaner
than the brooms we've had before."

"No, no!" the witch protested,
"I prefer a broom that's old,
like that one in the corner
with the noticeable mold."
"We were about to throw it out,"
the clerk replied, nonplussed.
"A broom like that would never do
to sweep up all your dust."

"Yes, yes!" she shrieked, and snatched it.
"It is mine at any cost.
It's practically the double
of the broom I said I'd lost."
The clerk said, "We deliver,
and can send it out today."
"No need!" she cackled, grinning,
and she flew that broom away.

A Place I've Always Known

There is a place I've always known,
a sort of secret hollow,
where only I may go alone,
and you may never follow.

Throughout the day, throughout the night,
that place is always there,
but though you search with all your might,
you'll find no thoroughfare.

You won't unearth it, though you look
beneath the salty sea,
atop a mountain, in a brook,
or by a leafy tree.

But I can find it easily,
and never need a guide. . . .
That place that's only known to me
is hidden deep inside.

Burt the Burper

Burt the Burper is my hero,
he's a burping superstar.
He can burp a small explosion,
or the engine of a car.
If there is a better burper,
I've not met that burper yet.
On a single moment's notice,
Burt can burp the alphabet.

I've heard many other burpers,
some of whom are pretty good.
They treat Burt with admiration
when he's in the neighborhood.
Burt burps longer, Burt burps louder
than all other burpers do.
I have known his burps to startle
bears and tigers at the zoo.

84

Burt's a burping virtuoso,
he's the best that's ever been.
When we have a burping contest,
it's a cinch that Burt will win.
When he burps with force and vigor,
he could make a demon scream—
at the fine old art of burping,
Burt the Burper reigns supreme.

The Laugh of the Luffer

The laugh of the Luffer is lovely,
and lively and lilting and long.
The sound of it makes you so happy,
you're likely to burst into song.

The laugh of the Luffer is luscious,
a glorious treat for the ears.
It fills you with feelings of gladness,
and instantly dries all your tears.

The laugh of the Luffer disguises
the Luffer's insidious goal,
and that is to lunge as you listen,
and suddenly swallow you whole.

So listen at length to the laughter,
but if it's too loud, that's your clue,
the Luffer grows closer . . . don't linger,
just leave lest the laugh is on you.

My Brother Poked a Porcupine

My brother poked a porcupine,
which was a great mistake.
My mother had hysterics
when she stumbled on a snake.
My sister fell into a creek,
she's cold and soaking wet.
My aunt upset a hornets' nest,
an act we all regret.

I sat in poison ivy,
I'll be itchy in a while.
A skunk sprayed both my uncles,
now they smell extremely vile.
My father stepped in something
he would rather not discuss—
we love our weekly nature walks,
they're always fun for us.

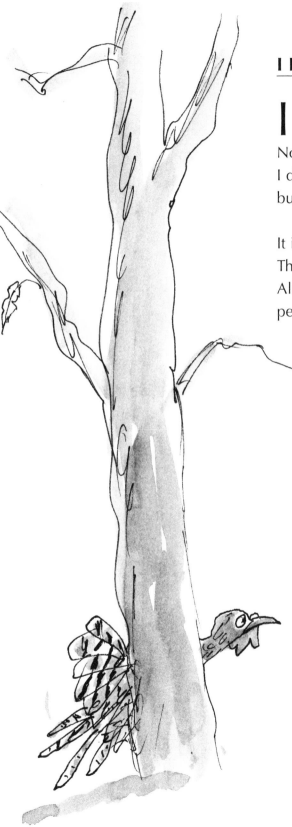

I Do Not Like November

I do not like November.
November is no fun.
I do not mind the other months,
but truly dread this one.

It is the month we celebrate
Thanksgiving in our land.
Alas, I am a turkey—
perhaps you understand.

Two Legendary Dragons

Two legendary dragons,
both of countrywide renown,
encountered one another,
neither dragon would back down.
They glared with pure malevolence,
for neither could disguise
it despised its mighty rival—
fury filled their fiery eyes.

They flared their giant nostrils,
they displayed their razor claws.
They roared with wild abandon,
and they snapped their fearsome jaws.
It was woefully apparent
they would always disagree
which possessed the greater prowess,
might, and sheer ferocity.

They snorted in defiance
as they called each other names,
and soon they were exhaling
inextinguishable flames.
The heat was overwhelming,
both ignited with a flash,
and those legendary dragons
were reduced to piles of ash.

I Never Sit on Scrambled Eggs

I never sit on scrambled eggs,
I know it isn't right.
I never swim in pudding,
it's considered impolite.
I never mash bananas
in my sister's curly hair,
and seldom stuff spaghetti
down my brother's underwear.

I do not dance in oatmeal,
it makes messes on the floor.
I do not juggle gelatin,
at least not anymore.
I do not swing at watermelons
with my baseball bat—
my mother says the things I do
are worse than all of that.

Some Chickens

Some chickens love running,
some chickens love jumping,
and some love to swim in the ocean.

These chickens possess
a remarkable trait—
each one is pure poultry in motion.

The Geese Are Honking

The geese are honking all day long.
They honk and honk, for they've no song.
Their honking carries far and wide—
I guess those geese have horns inside.

Today It's Pouring Pythons

Today it's pouring pythons,
they're giving me a pain.
It's also raining boas,
as you may ascertain.

They're falling on the ballpark,
and that's why I complain.
A notice has been posted—
GAME CALLED . . . ANACONDA RAIN.

A Worm

A worm wends its winding and unaware way,
wiggling in solitude, day after day,
spending its life in the dark underground,
never emitting an audible sound.

It comes and it goes without purpose or aim,
for when you're a worm, every day is the same.
A wiggle, a wriggle, a squiggle, a squirm . . .
that's just about all that there is to a worm.

He Thought He Saw a Crocodile

He thought he saw a crocodile,
but it was just a frog.
He pointed to a hippo
that turned out to be a log.

He spied a pterodactyl
that was nothing but a kite,
then thought he saw a dinosaur—
We miss him . . . he was right.

Look! Look!

Look! Look!
A book!
A book for me,
a book all filled
with poetry,
a book that I
can read
and read.
A book!
Exactly
what I need.

Look! Look!
A book
to open wide,
and marvel
at the words inside,
to sit
and savor
quietly.
Look! Look!
A book!
A book for me.

The Snoober

The Snoober has eleven heads,
eleven legs on which it treads,
eleven tails, eleven eyes
to watch the world and scan the skies.

The Snoober has eleven wings,
eleven songs it often sings
with all of its eleven beaks . . .
the Snoober lives eleven weeks.

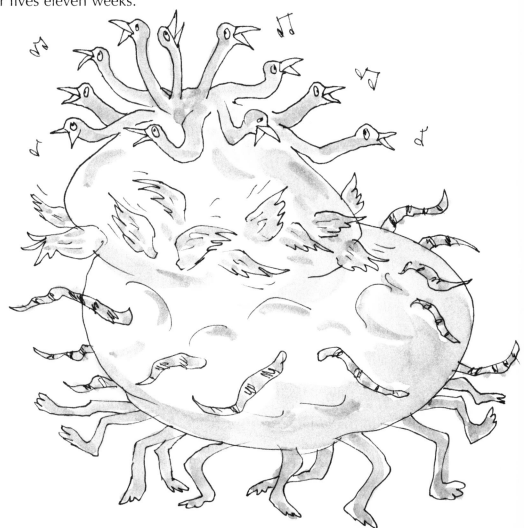

I'm Falling through a Funnel

I'm falling through a funnel, and it isn't any fun. I
wonder how I got in here, I wish that I were done.
Not only am I falling, I am swirling constantly. A funnel isn't somewhere that I'd
ever choose to be. I'm dropping ever
faster, I can't curb my swift descent.
This day is not the finest day that I
have ever spent. I cannot
seem to stop myself, I
have a sense of woe,
and now I'm falling
really fast,
and
now
I've
s
t
o
p
p
e
d
.
.
.
HELLO!

A Problem with the Probbles

A problem with the Probbles
is their total lack of tact.
They're positively impolite,
they don't know how to act.
They're apt to blurt out sentences
you'd rather never hear,
like "You've got ugly pimples!"
and "Your nose looks like an ear!"

A problem with the Probbles
is their aggravating yell.
They're, furthermore, malodorous,
you will not like their smell.
They're truly reprehensible,
their breath is far from sweet.
They love to stomp on tender toes—
they have enormous feet.

A problem with the Probbles
is their paucity of grace.
They make repugnant gestures,
and they sneeze into your face.
They constantly expectorate,
they are a dreadful clan.
It's best to keep your distance
from the Probbles . . . if you can.

I've Made a Spectacular Necktie

I've made a spectacular necktie,
a beautiful Father's Day gift.
I know that he's going to love it,
I'm sure it will give him a lift.
He doesn't have anything like it,
I'm certain it's one of a kind . . .
it may be the very best necktie
that anyone's ever designed.

I've painted his necktie with pictures
of orange and indigo trees,
a rainbow arrangement of flowers,
and seventeen green bumblebees.
I hardly can wait till he sees it,
he'll be so delighted he'll roar—
I bet that he wears it more often
than neckties I've made him before.

I'm Appearing Out of Nowhere

I'm appearing out of nowhere,
I'm beginning to exist.
I had never been an inkling,
not a whisper in a mist.
I've been absolutely nothing
for as long as I recall,
now I'm fast becoming something
where I'd never been at all.

It's bewildering to fathom
how this change is taking place,
why I now develop substance
where there'd never been a trace.
Since I'd never had a being,
having one feels rather strange.
Nonetheless, I'm quite enchanted
by this unexpected change.

Where I'd long been unapparent
in an empty, vast abyss,
now I reach the culmination
of my metamorphosis.
With each single passing second
I grow easier to see,
and my consciousness increases . . .
I am turning into me.

My Sister's Taking Lessons

My sister's taking lessons
in learning how to sing.
From everything I've heard so far,
she hasn't learned a thing.
It hurts my ears to listen
when she tries to sing a song. . . .
For every note that she gets right,
she gets a dozen wrong.

Her voice is sort of scratchy,
and she's always out of tune.
I think I'd rather listen
to an ostrich or baboon.
Her teacher keeps insisting
she's improving every day—
unless she sounds much better soon,
I'm moving far away.

When the Butcher Was Delivered

When the butcher was delivered,
and the tailor was disclosed,
the sculptor was disfigured,
and his models were deposed.
The painter was discolored,
and the laundress was depressed,
the jockey was dismounted,
and the barber was distressed.

The doctors lost their patience,
the perfumers had no sense,
the bankers had no interest,
but the clowns remained intense.
The mailman was unlettered,
and the poet was reversed,
the tailor was unseemly,
and the butcher feared the worst.

The sailors were deported,
and the cobblers were unsold,
the actors all departed,
and the bakers were unrolled.
The fishermen were reeling,
and the bellmen were repealed,
the tailor was in stitches,
and the butcher was revealed.

I Love When Someone Whistles

I love when someone whistles,
when someone sings or hums.
I love the clash of cymbals,
the *rump-a-tump* of drums.
I love to hear a violin,
a cello, or a bass.
When someone toots a flute,
a smile illuminates my face.

I love the sound of trumpets,
of mellow slide trombones,
of high-pitched fifes and piccolos,
and booming sousaphones.
There hardly is a better way
to spend an afternoon,
than listening intently
to an oboe or bassoon.

I love a ukulele,
the blare of big brass bands,
and when I hear a clarinet,
I have to clap my hands.
A banjo or a tambourine
can fill me with delight—
if you think I love music,
I think you may be right.

The Average Hippopotamus

The average hippopotamus
is big from top to bottomus,
it travels at a trotamus,
and swims when days are hotamus.

Because it eats a lotamus,
it's practically a yachtamus,
so it's a cinch to spotamus
the average hippopotamus.

I Have a Lamb

I have a lamb
that loves to dance,
it dances every day,
and every time
it has a chance,
it practices *baaaaa*-let.

I Am Climbing Up a Ladder

NOW I'M
MY BALANCE,
TO LOSE
I'VE BEGUN
TO SPIN AROUND.
THINGS APPEAR
SLIGHTLY DIZZY,
BUT I'M GETTING
STAY AWARE.
YOU HAD BETTER
THIS UNSTEADY,
ON A LADDER
EXTRA CARE.
SO I'M TAKING
SLIGHTLY SHAKING,
NOW THIS LADDER'S
TAKE YOUR TIME.
IT IS BEST TO
UP A LADDER,
WHEN YOU'RE GOING
AS I RESOLUTELY CLIMB.
MOVEMENT
WATCH MY EVERY
I MUST
WANT TO FALL.
FOR I DO NOT
REALLY CAUTIOUS,
SO I'M BEING
VERY TALL,
AND THE LADDER'S
UP A LADDER,
AM CLIMBING

WHOOPS!   *BACK*

O

N

T

H

E

GROUND!

I'm Glad I'm Me

I'm glad I'm me, I'm glad I'm me,
there's no one else I want to be.
I'm happy I'm the person who
can do the things that I can do.

If I were someone else, then I
would feel so strange, I'd wonder why.
I'm positive that I'd be sad—
but I *am* me, and I am glad.

My Hobby Is Unusual

My hobby is unusual,
for I collect squashed bugs.
I hunt them in the garden,
I seek them under rugs.
I find them in the kitchen,
a place they often are.
I snatch them with my fingers,
and I drop them in a jar.

I'm certain I've collected
quite a sizeable amount.
I've no idea how many . . .
I long ago lost count.
I only know I catch them all
by sneaking up behind them.
And oh, there's just one other thing—
they're not squashed when I find them.

Why Can't They Be Quiet?

Why can't they be quiet,
those cats, those cats,
instead of engaging
in quarrels and spats?
Why must they howl
in such horrible tones,
filling the air
with their miserable moans?

Why do they caterwaul,
why do they fight,
waking the neighborhood
night after night?
Why must they be
such cantankerous brats?
Why can't they be quiet,
those cats, those cats?

Sprig Id Here

Sprig id here,
I hab a code.
Idz id duh biddu
ub by dode.
Idz id duh biddu
ub by head.
I'b bidderabu,
add I'b id bed.

I caddod breed,
I caddod smell.
I sneed and sneed,
I ab dod well,
add yed my hard
id fidd wid cheer …
I hab a code,
bud sprig id here.

The Spells & Smells Motel

We witches love our weekends
at the Spells & Smells Motel.
They cultivate our business,
and they treat our coven well.
The sparse accommodations
are appropriately grim.
The faucets won't stop dripping,
and the lights are always dim.

The rooms are dank and gloomy,
every mirror has a crack,
the unattractive furniture
is painted ghastly black.
The sofas are uncomfortable,
the chairs are missing legs,
the cushions' pungent odor
is a lot like rotten eggs.

The curtains are unsightly,
and the carpets are a fright,
aswarm with noxious insects
that keep biting day and night.
There's dust in every corner,
ancient cobwebs overhead,
and lumpy bumpy mattresses
on every wretched bed.

Outside the broken windows,
creepy creatures moan and howl,
the Continental breakfast
tastes unmentionably foul.
They even sprinkle henbane
in our complimentary tea,
and around-the-clock broom service
is both courteous and free.

The Blue-Bean-Bonking Bupple

In a weird machine, unheard, unseen,
lives the blue-bean-bonking Bupple,
whose tentacles are long and lean,
and sinuous and supple.

The Bupple's wily, slick, and sly,
and from that weird machine,
it shrewdly bonks all passersby
with a big blue bonking bean.

Although those beans don't hurt a bit,
there's something worse they do.
Those beans deposit, where they hit,
a dollop of blue goo.

So stay away from the weird machine
of the blue-bean-bonking Bupple,
or you'll be bonked by a big blue bean,
and possibly a couple.

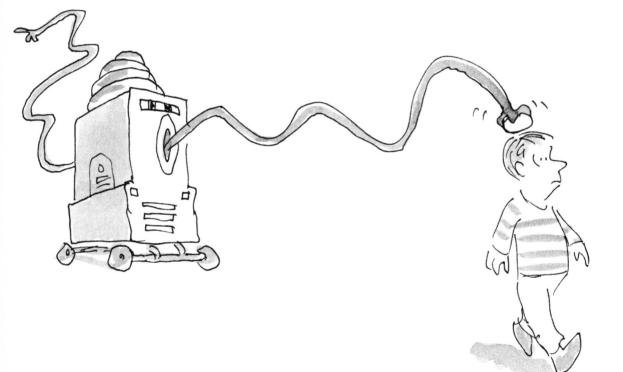

Song of the Lizard Lovers

Lizard, oh lizard, we love you, we do.
There's no finer reptile to nibble or chew.
No toad ever tickled our taste buds like you.
Lizard, oh lizard, we love you, we do.

We love eating lizard, so savory and sweet.
A meal without lizard is quite incomplete.
We love lizard sizzled in onions and oil,
we love lizard simmered, or brought to a boil.

Lizard, oh lizard, we love you, we do.
There's no finer reptile to nibble or chew.
No toad ever tickled our taste buds like you.
Lizard, oh lizard, we love you, we do.

We love lizard gizzard, we love lizard legs,
we love lizard pickled, or scrambled with eggs.
We love lizard casserole, lizard on rye,
tongue of raw lizard still stuck to a fly.

Lizard, oh lizard, we love you, we do.
There's no finer reptile to nibble or chew.
No toad ever tickled our taste buds like you.
Lizard, oh lizard, we love you, we do.

We love munching lizard with carrots and peas,
slathered with ketchup, or dripping with cheese.
We love lizard dumplings, and lizard flambé . . .
there's nothing like lizard to brighten our day.

Lizard, oh lizard, we love you, we do.
There's no finer reptile to nibble or chew.
No toad ever tickled our taste buds like you.
Lizard, oh lizard, we love you, we do.

The Preposterous Wosstrus

I am the preposterous Wosstrus
that sleeps in the back of your mind.
It takes but a thought to revive me,
and so I'm no trouble to find.
Sometimes I'm as big as a hippo,
sometimes I'm as small as a flea.
Depending on how you command me,
I'm just what you want me to be.

I am the preposterous Wosstrus,
invisible, yet always near.
I'll hurry as soon as you call me,
just summon me and I'll appear.
I'm with you for ever and ever.
You never can leave me behind—
I am the preposterous Wosstrus
that sleeps in the back of your mind.

The Mockingbird Is Famous

The mockingbird is famous
for its variable voice.
Unlike most birds, whose notes are few,
it has abundant choice.
It finds it dull to simply sing
one single song alone,
and pilfers songs from other birds,
then treats them as its own.

No matter how another bird
may cackle, coo, or croon,
the mockingbird is capable
of copying the tune.
Although this virtuosity
makes it a singing star,
the mockingbird owes everything
to borrowed repertoire.

WAAKA WOK

WAAKA WOK

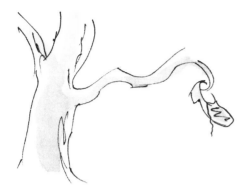

I Picked Up a Pebble

I picked up a pebble,
and started to rock.
A tree took my shoe,
so I gave it a sock.
My bat flew away,
I was tempted to bawl.
My belt had no holes,
so I gave it my all.

A raven craved candy,
a crow had a bar.
The bottles were gone,
but the door was ajar.
An orca was sad,
and proceeded to wail.
The shovel was missing,
the bucket looked pale.

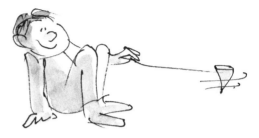

My rabbits were shaggy,
I combed every hare.
I found some bananas,
and swallowed a pair.
My mom gave me soda,
I drank all the pop,
then sat on my bottom
while spinning my top.

Eureka! Hooray!

Eureka! Hooray! I've invented
a thing that's entirely unique,
a truly inspired contraption
I've worked on for nearly a week.
It's roughly the size of a blender,
and roughly the shape of a squid.
I'm truly amazed that I made it,
and can't quite believe that I did.

To make my mechanical marvel,
I had to rely on my brains.
I took a few parts from my robot,
my glider, my cars, and my trains.
I borrowed a couple of lightbulbs,
a phone, and a shower massage,
and some miscellaneous items
my father keeps in the garage.

The kitchen produced a bonanza
of ladles and funnels and forks,
plus other assorted utensils,
as well as a couple of corks.
I needed the spoon and the strainer
my mother likes using for rice—
it takes an array of components
to build a creative device.

I fit all the pieces together,
which wasn't too easy to do.
I hammered in nails by the hundred,
and squeezed out a river of glue.
I still have two problems remaining,
which I can't pretend to ignore . . .
I can't figure out how to start it,
and have no idea what it's for.

133

The Flaky Corn Brigade

We are the husky members
of the **FLAKY CORN BRIGADE**.
We march about in earnest
on continual parade.
We march in rows on cobblestones,
we march through field and mall.
We munch on muffins, beef, and bread,
and always have a ball.

We are chipper, we are gritty,
never mushy, never meek.
In fact, we're so amazing,
we believe we are unique.
We are copious in number
as we march across the land.
We are the **FLAKY CORN BRIGADE**—
our colonel's in command.

Chirpers Chirp and Cheepers Cheep

Chirpers chirp and cheepers cheep,
burpers burp and beepers beep
early, early on my lawn—
that is why I'm up at dawn.

When My Father Grew a Mustache

When my father grew a mustache,
it came as a surprise.
It was extremely bushy,
and reached a splendid size.

He combed that mustache daily,
he watered it a lot,
and so that mustache flourished
in my father's flowerpot.

I'm Trapped in an Egg

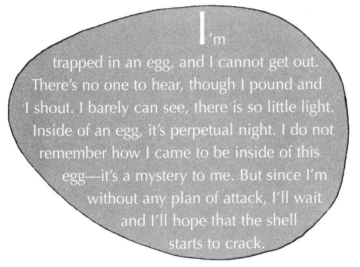

I'm trapped in an egg, and I cannot get out. There's no one to hear, though I pound and I shout. I barely can see, there is so little light. Inside of an egg, it's perpetual night. I do not remember how I came to be inside of this egg—it's a mystery to me. But since I'm without any plan of attack, I'll wait and I'll hope that the shell starts to crack.

The Monster Museum

The Monster Museum is open today,
come in, everybody, come in.
You're sure to be frightened by every display,
we promise to tingle your skin.

Our courteous monsters (we have quite a few)
are waiting to cordially greet you.
No other museum can do what we do,
for here the exhibits might eat you.

This Morning

This morning is, decidedly,
exceptionally weird.
My favorite rhinoceros
has grown a golden beard.

Though I'm unsure how this occurred,
and don't know what to do,
my rhinoceros seems happy,
so I guess I'm happy too.

The Violinnets and Celloons

The Violinnets and Celloons
are birds designed to play
a medley of engaging tunes
for hours and hours a day.
Their music carries on the breeze
and drifts across the lake . . .
you'll love the dulcet harmonies
these virtuosi make.

You'll love the way their stirring sound
will waft into your ears.
Their melodies are so profound,
you may be moved to tears.
Don't wait another minute,
call and place your order soon
for a graceful Violinnet,
and an elegant Celloon.

I'm Dancing with My Elephants

I'm dancing with my elephants,
a scintillating treat.
They're both extremely graceful,
light and limber on their feet.
They move with ease and elegance
and glide across the floor.
I'm dancing with my elephants . . .
how could I ask for more?

They effortlessly pirouette,
then leap into the air.
A crowd looks on in wonder
at this sight beyond compare.
And when they spin and somersault,
the crowd erupts and roars.
I'm dancing with my elephants—
I hope you dance with yours.

I Am Loudmouse

I am Loudmouse, and by far,
loudest of all mice that are,
of all mice that ever were,
of all mice that might occur.

Surely there will never be
another mouse as loud as me.
I am utterly unique . . .
I am Loudmouse, hear me squeak!

I'm Going to the Library

I'm going to the library,
and moving very slow,
despite the fact that it's a place
I've always liked to go.
But I'm not looking forward now
to being there at all,
and that is why I'm heading there
at practically a crawl.

I'm going to the library,
and I'm a bit afraid.
It's all because of one mistake
I've accidentally made.
I'm filled with trepidation
mixed with downright misery,
convinced that the librarian
is furious with me.

I know that I'm in trouble,
so I'm in a frantic state.
I also know it's all my fault,
and I deserve my fate.
I'm going to the library,
and shaking through and through—
the book I'm finally bringing back
is four years overdue.

The Sun Is Setting in the West

The sun is setting in the west,
it sets there every day.
If it starts setting somewhere else,
then I will move away.

My Brother's Invisible Dragon

My brother's invisible dragon
is practically always around.
It's roughly the size of a rhino,
and doesn't make much of a sound.
My brother insists that his dragon
has scales of indelible green.
I wonder how he knows the color
of something that cannot be seen.

I've never been able to spy it,
it won't show itself to my eyes,
so when I bump into that dragon,
it's always an awkward surprise.
My brother's invisible dragon
possesses a mischievous flair.
It burns my dessert every evening—
that's why I'm convinced that it's there.

Mister Lauder's Brilliant Daughter

Mister Lauder's brilliant daughter
has invented instant water,
little crystals, white and pink—
just add water, stir, and drink.

I Have a Pet Orangutan

I have a pet orangutan,
the two of us play chess.
I always won when we began,
but now I'm winning less.
He's learning from experience
to beat me at this game.
I cannot quite keep up with him,
my skill remains the same.

His strategy grows stronger,
and he's making better moves.
He almost never blunders,
every day his game improves.
So though I do not like it,
I admit, reluctantly,
it's apparent my orangutan
is cleverer than me.

What Do I Do with a Gremlin?

What do I do with a gremlin
that regularly misbehaves,
a gremlin whose ways are unseemly,
a gremlin that rages and raves,
a gremlin that wears my pajamas,
and callously shaves off my hair,
a gremlin that uses my crayons
to color my new underwear?

What do I do with a gremlin
that's usually up to no good,
a gremlin that snatches my homework,
and hides it away in its hood,
a gremlin that raises a racket
whenever I'm trying to doze,
a gremlin inclined to take feathers,
and impishly tickle my toes?

What do I do with a gremlin
that does all it can to displease,
a gremlin that peppers my pillow,
and covers my mattress with cheese,
a gremlin that swings from the ceiling,
and wears an unpleasant perfume,
a crude and obstreperous gremlin
that thinks it belongs in my room?

I Began to Blow a Bubble

I began to blow a bubble
with a dozen sticks of gum.
The bubble wasn't big enough,
and so I added some.
The bubble soon grew bigger,
but I wasn't satisfied,
I opened up much wider
and I stuffed more gum inside.

I chewed and chewed
and chewed and chewed
and chewed and chewed still more.
I blew a bigger bubble
than I'd ever blown before.
That bubble kept on growing,
it was bigger than my head,
but I blew and blew that bubble
as my face turned cherry red.

That bubble grew gigantic,
it was fifty feet around.
Then suddenly it lifted me
directly off the ground.
I'm rising high above the clouds,
and don't know when I'll stop—
I hope and hope with all my heart
my bubble doesn't pop.

Index to Titles

Index to First Lines